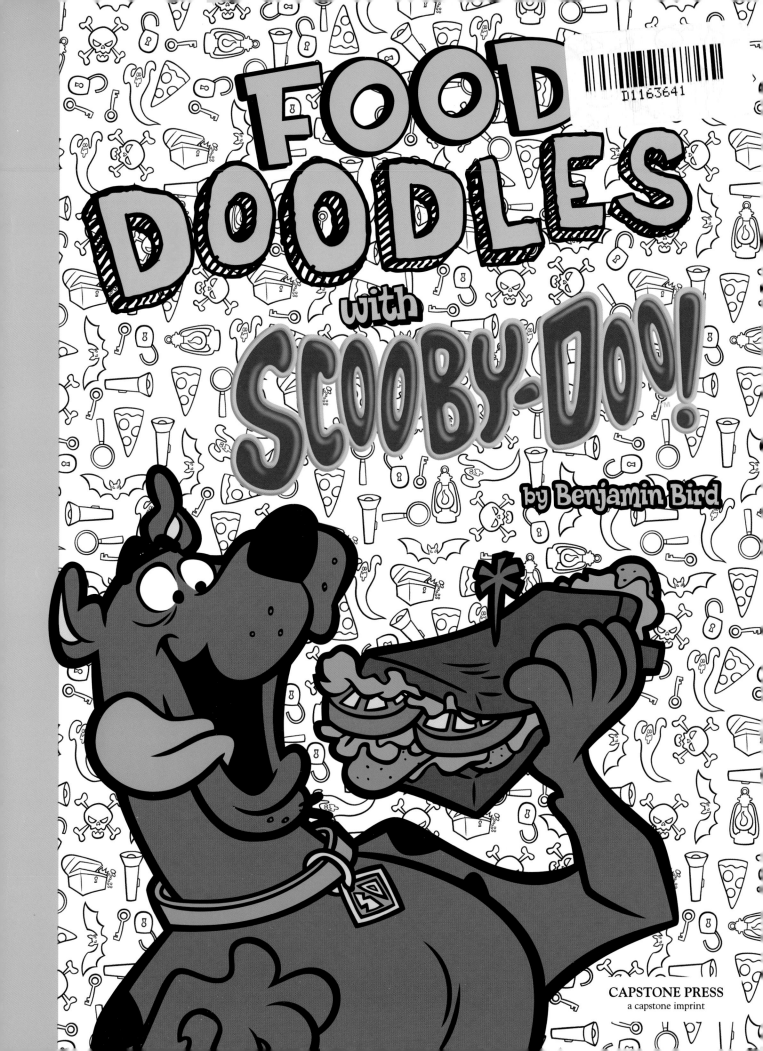

# FOOD DOODLES
## with
# SCOOBY-DOO!

by Benjamin Bird

CAPSTONE PRESS
a capstone imprint

Scooby-Doodles
are published in 2017 by Stone Arch Books,
A Capstone Imprint
1710 Roe Crest Drive,
North Mankato, Minnesota 56003
www.mycapstone.com

CAPS38616

Cataloging-in-Publication Data is available on the Library of Congress website.

ISBN: 978-1-5157-3407-9 (hardcover)
ISBN: 978-1-5157-3412-3 (eBook)

Summary: Draw and create FOOD doodles with Scooby-Doo!

Designed by Lori Bye

Capstone Studio: Karon Dubke, (supplies) 5; Scott Neely: (sketches) 8-9, 10-11,
12, 16-17, 18-19, 20-21, 23, 25, 27, 29.

All other illustrations not listed above are credits to Warner Brothers

# TABLE OF CONTENTS

# LIKE, HELP, SCOOBS!

Zoinks! Think art is truly terrifying? Well, think again.

Like solving a great mystery, drawing just takes a little planning and practice. In *Food Doodles with Scooby-Doo!*, you'll discover tools, tips, and tricks to make doodling a totally delicious experience.

Use this book for daily doodling fun! In your own sketchbook, follow Scooby and the gang through warm-up exercises, pattern practice, and step-by-step drawing instructions.

You'll unmask your inner artist in no time!

# TOOLS

Scooby and the gang need proper tools, like flashlights and magnifying glasses, to solve mysteries. With a few basic tools, you can doodle like a pro!

## ERASER

Ruh-roh! Don't fear mistakes. An eraser can solve most problems.

## RULER

Even the shakiest hand can draw a straight line with a ruler.

## PENCILS

Jinkies! Worried about making mistakes? Sketch outlines of your doodles first. They're great for detailed coloring, too!

## FINE-TIP MARKERS

Any great detective knows details matter — the same goes for great doodlers! Use fine-tip, waterproof markers to give your drawings scary-good details.

## COLORED MARKERS

Don't get lost in the dark! Brighten up your doodles with multicolored markers.

# MEET MYSTERY INC.

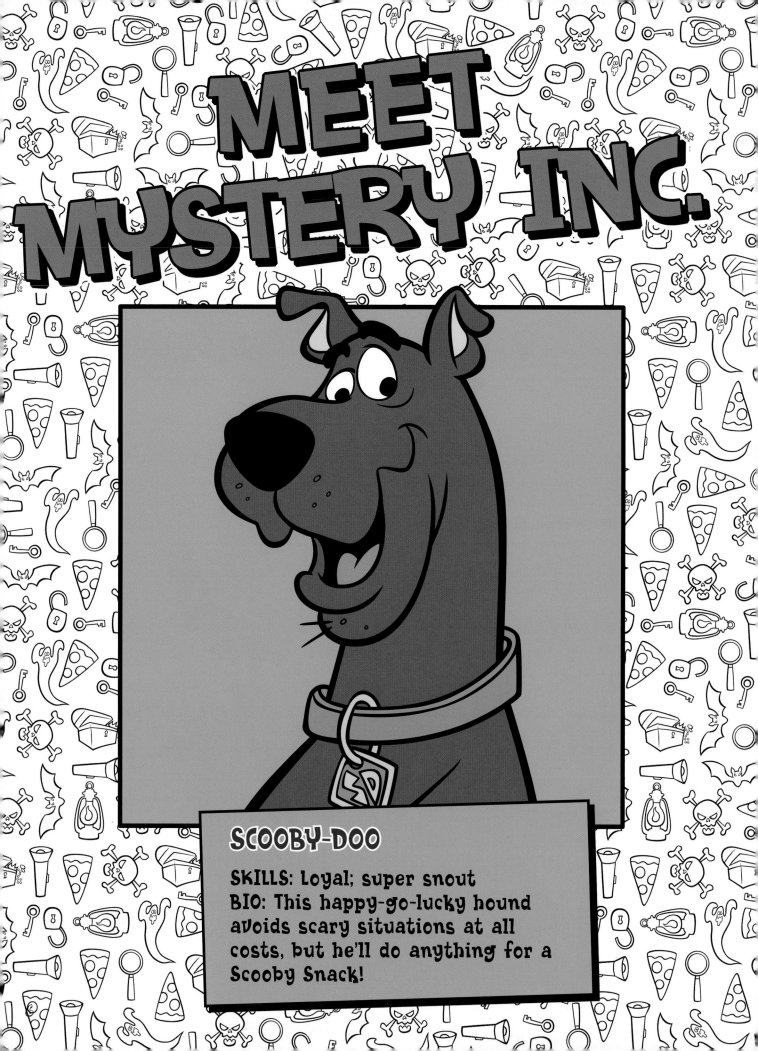

## SCOOBY-DOO

SKILLS: Loyal; super snout
BIO: This happy-go-lucky hound avoids scary situations at all costs, but he'll do anything for a Scooby Snack!

## SHAGGY ROGERS

**SKILLS:** Lucky; healthy appetite
**BIO:** This laid-back dude would rather look for grub than search for clues, but he usually finds both!

## FRED JONES, JR.

**SKILLS:** Athletic; charming
**BIO:** The leader and oldest member of the gang. He's a good sport — and good at them, too!

## DAPHNE BLAKE

**SKILLS:** Brains; beauty
**BIO:** As a sixteen-year-old fashion queen, Daphne solves her mysteries in style.

## VELMA DINKLEY

**SKILLS:** Clever; highly intelligent
**BIO:** Although she's the youngest member of Mystery Inc., Velma's an old pro at catching crooks.

# GANGWAY!

Scooby-Doo and Shaggy would never start a meal without an appetizer! Use these bite-sized exercises to kickoff your doodling feast.

In your sketchbook, doodle as many STINKY FOODS as you can in five minutes!

In your sketchbook, doodle all of these

SPICY SNACKS,

and then create some of your own!

# DISCOVER PATTERNS

To crack a case, great detectives look for patterns of evidence. Doodling patterns — repeating the same design over and over — can help you discover your path to drawing success.

IN YOUR SKETCHBOOK, DOODLE THIS PATTERN OF DELECTABLE FOODS. OR, CREATE ONE OF YOUR OWN!

Draw as many circle-shaped foods as you can imagine.
Then create delicious patterns from other food shapes!

# SNACK-TIVITY!

Notice any patterns in your own diet?
Here's an easy way to find out!

1. Carry a sketchbook to each meal for a week.

2. Using a pencil, sketch every meal you eat.

3. At the end of the week, search for patterns in the foods you've eaten. Did you eat a lot of spicy foods? Sweet foods? Salty foods? Take note.

4. Then try this Snack-tivity again and see if you notice any changes from week to week!

RUMMY!

# FIND CLUES

Scooby and the gang focus on finding small clues to solve big mysteries. Grid drawing is a great way to break a large illustration into smaller, more manageable parts.

**TOOLS:**
Ruler
Pencil
Paper
Fine-tip marker
Eraser

1. Using the ruler and pencil, draw a grid of squares like the one on page 15 (five columns and seven rows).

2. Next, choose a square of Scooby to draw with the fine-tip marker.

3. Once you've finished drawing one square, start on another. And then another and another!

4. When you've finished drawing all the squares, use the eraser to remove the grid from your Scooby drawing!

# IT'S A RIZZA RARTY!

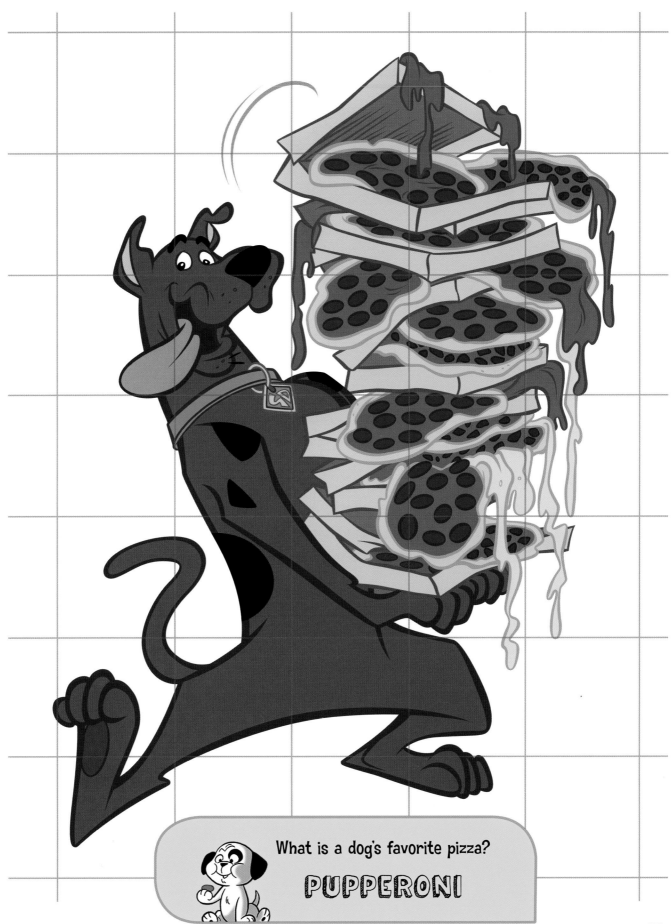

What is a dog's favorite pizza?

PUPPERONI

# FOLLOW LEADS

The Mystery Inc. gang follows a series of leads, or clues, to solve every case. In the pages to come, follow each series of instructions to create groovy drawings.

# SCOOBY!

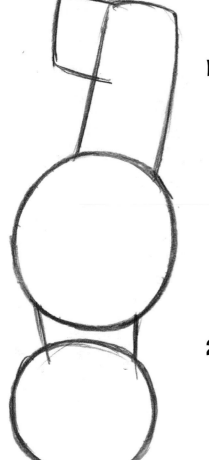

1. With a pencil, lightly outline the main shapes of Scooby's body and head.

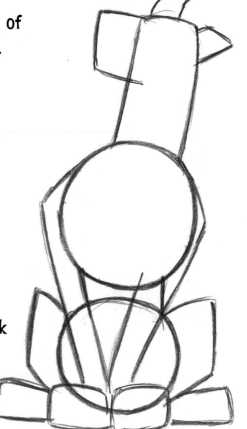

2. Using the outline as your guide, draw Scooby's front and back legs. Add his ears, too!

3. Then, give Scooby some details! Add his eyes, eyebrows, mouth, and dog tag. Afterward, erase any unnecessary lines and fix any last-minute mistakes.

4. ADD COLOR!
   Outline your drawing with a fine-tip, black marker. Then use colored markers to bring Scooby to life!

NOW HOW ABOUT A SCOOBY SNACK?

# MYSTERY MACHINE FOOD TRUCK!

Sometimes the Mystery Inc. gang uses the Mystery Machine to go undercover to solve a mystery. Today, the gang transforms their van into a food truck to trap a hungry fiend. Draw your own food truck in a few simple steps!

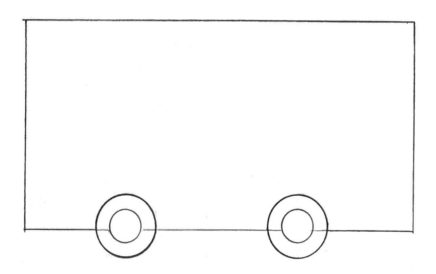

1. Difficult drawings often begin with simple shapes. To create the Mystery Machine, begin by lightly sketching a large rectangle. Then draw two sets of circles for the van's tires.

2. Using the rectangle shape as your guide, draw an outline of the van. Add a window, bumper, and wheel wells to your Mystery Machine.

**3.** Next, add details to the van, such as a roof rack, steering wheel, and passenger-side door.

**4.** Finish off your Mystery Machine with far-out decorations, like flowers and wheels. Don't be afraid — be creative! Follow the example at left, or create a brand-new design for your van!

**5.** Finally, using colored pencils or markers, give the Mystery Machine a custom food truck look!

SCOOBY'S HOT DOG TRUCK

LIKE WOW!

# Have a case of ARTISTIC BRAIN FREEZE?

Here's a sweet trick . . . Doodle a supersized ice-cream cone that even Scooby couldn't finish!

# CAKE CONE!

1. Begin your cake cone by identifying the basic shapes.. Remember: sketch lightly with a pencil at first! You can always erase any unnecessary lines or mistakes later on.

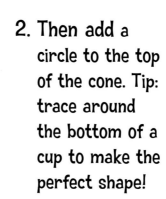

2. Then add a circle to the top of the cone. Tip: trace around the bottom of a cup to make the perfect shape!

3. Using the circle shape as your guide, draw the swirls of your ice cream. Add lines to the base of your cone. Use a ruler to make straight lines, if desired.

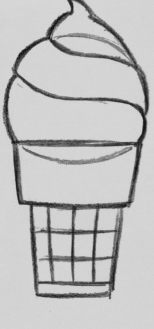

4. Finally, erase any unnecessary lines and finish with sprinkles!

# SUGAR CONE!

1. Difficult drawings often begin with simple shapes. To create a sugar cone, begin by lightly sketching a triangle.

2. Next add a scoop of ice cream to the top of your triangle cone.

3. Don't be shy! Draw a second scoop on top!

4. Finish with a cherry on top! Outline your drawing with a fine-tip, black marker. Then fill in the cone with any color you prefer!

SCOOBY DOOBY DOO!

# SCOOBY SNACKS!

Scooby Snacks are Scooby-Doo's favorite treat!

Doodle a Scooby Snack box using the steps on the next page. Then give the box an appetizing new design!

1. Begin your Scooby Snack box by drawing a rectangle.

2. Next add short lines to three corners of your rectangle, like the image below.

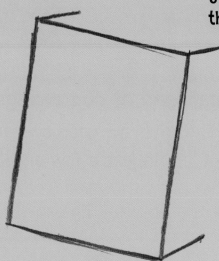

3. Then connect the short lines to make your box three-dimensional.

4. Finish your Scooby Snack box with a groovy new design. And, of course, add a few tasty treats to go with it!

WOULD YOU DO IT FOR A SCOOBY SNACK?

# HOT DOG!

What kind of dog always runs a fever?
A hot dog! Draw your own foot-long frankfurter
in just a few simple steps!

1. With a pencil, lightly sketch the basic shape of your hot dog. This same shape will be used for both sides of the bun, too!

2. Draw a similar, smaller shape in front of your hot dog for the bun. Erase any unnecessary lines as you go.

3. Next add the other side of the hot dog bun, using the previous shapes as your guide.

4. ADD COLOR!
Outline your drawing with a fine-tip, black marker. Then fill in the hot dog with any color you prefer!

THEN...
Cover the hot dog with toppings, or sign your name in mustard!

# BURGER TIME!

Draw this ooey-gooey hamburger, and then add even more tasty toppings!

1. Begin by drawing the top bun of your hamburger.

2. Next, add a few toppings, like lettuce, tomatoes, and cheese.

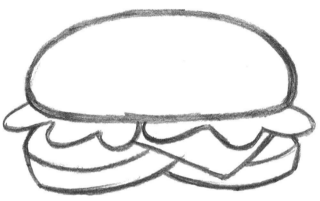

3. Then, add the hamburger patty and bottom bun. At this point, begin to customize your burger. Want mushrooms? Jalapeños? Bacon? The choice is up to you!

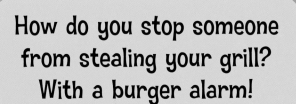

4. Finally, outline your burger with a fine-tip marker and color!

How do you stop someone from stealing your grill? With a burger alarm!

Ever dream of owning your own restaurant?
Now's your chance! In your sketchbook, practice doodling the
restaurant logos below, and then create your own!

SCOOBY-DOO
**Famous Restaurant**

Scooby-Doo Cafe

Scooby-Doo Approved!
HOT DOG
SD

## Benjamin Bird

Benjamin Bird is a children's book editor and freelance writer from St. Paul, Minnesota. He has written books about some of today's most popular characters, including Batman, Superman, Wonder Woman, Scooby-Doo, Tom & Jerry, and many more.

## Scott Neely

Scott Neely has been a professional illustrator and designer for many years. Since 1999, he's been an official Scooby-Doo and Cartoon Network artist, working on such licensed properties as Dexter's Laboratory, Johnny Bravo, Courage The Cowardly Dog, Powerpuff Girls, and more. He has also worked on Pokemon, Mickey Mouse Clubhouse, My Friends Tigger & Pooh, Handy Manny, Strawberry Shortcake, Bratz, and many other popular characters. He lives in a suburb of Philadelphia and has a scrappy Yorkshire Terrier, Alfie.

# Are you thinking what I'm thinking?

## Discover more

# SCOOBY-DOODLES!

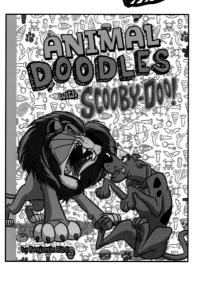

**Only from Capstone!**

The fun doesn't stop here!

Discover more at...
www.CapstoneKids.com

Find cool websites and more
books like this one at
www.Facthound.com.
Just type in the
BOOK ID: 9781515734079
and you're ready to go!